The Thriller

By the mid 1940s, the last six-shooting, cigar-smoking gangster had hung up his Hollywood Homburg. Directors seeking a new realism, a new way of keeping the audiences on the edge of their seats, began to make suspense thrillers — and inadvertently discovered the formula that was to keep box office takings healthy for over thirty years. In concise text and over 100 illustrations, Brian Davis traces the metamorphosis of this extraordinarily popular *genre*, from the 'new realism' of films like *The House on 92nd Street* and *Naked City* to the gritty crime thrillers and superspy extravaganzas of the present day. Two of the thriller film's key motifs, the robbery and the chase, are examined in detail; films using the classic thriller framework to examine social and political problems — such as *Crossfire*, *Victim*, *Z*, *The Manchurian Candidate* — are discussed in depth; and so are films like *Cul-de-Sac* and *Mickey One*, which adapt this classic framework for their own surrealistic ends.

The Thriller is a lively and provocative introduction to its subject.

Brian Davis

The Thriller

the suspense film from 1946

Studio Vista | Dutton Pictureback

Cover illustrations

Front cover William Friedkin's *The French Connection* (1971). Gene Heickman and Marcel Bozzufi
Back cover Gordon Parks's *Shaft's Big Score* (1972). Richard Roundtree

© Brian Davis 1973
Published in Great Britain by Studio Vista
Blue Star House, Highgate Hill, London N19
and in the USA by E.P. Dutton and Co., Inc.
201 Park Avenue South, New York, NY 10003
Set in Univers 689 9D on 12pt
Made and printed in Great Britain by
Richard Clay (The Chaucer Press), Ltd, Bungay, Suffolk

ISBN 0 289 70341 7 (paperback)
          0 289 70342 5 (hardback)

Contents

Introduction   7
The New Realism   9
The Private Eye   22
The Spy   36
Thrillers with a Message   55
The Chase   74
The *Psycho* Syndrome   101
The Heist   120
Other Parts of the Forest   140
Conclusion   154
Index   156

Introduction

In Alfred Hitchcock's definitive comedy-thriller, *North by Northwest* (1959), Cary Grant, the innocent advertising executive suspected of being a spy, is tricked into arranging a rendezvous in the deserted fields outside Chicago. The tranquil midsummer setting is occasionally disturbed by a crop-dusting plane buzzing lazily around the sunlit fields. As a passer-by notes, without much interest, its presence seems rather curious since there are no crops in the area. Suddenly, the plane changes direction, approaches Grant and opens fire.

By setting the scene in broad daylight and in peaceful surroundings, Hitchcock subtly disturbs the audience's preconceptions. In the cinema, people are supposed to be killed at night, in a dark alley, with a black cat lurking somewhere around the corner. He bends the rules again, and to more scarifying effect, in *Psycho* (1960), when an attractive young thief (Janet Leigh), the only character with whom the audience can identify, meets a peculiarly unpleasant fate in a motel shower. The film, abruptly and unnervingly, goes off on an entirely different tack.

Similarly, many post-1960 films by other directors bend or even reverse the established rules, which adds a new dimension to the suspense as the audience no longer knows whether the hero will triumph or whether the safecrackers will necessarily be foiled. In the more innocent days of the film thriller, it was a racing certainty that the hero would never be killed; that the bank robbers would walk into a trap through either bad luck or incompetence; and that someone who looked remarkably like Pearl White would be rescued by the clean-cut hero before the 9 : 40 to Buffalo steamed over her panting body.

Most of the thrillers discussed in this survey — which excludes the conventional gangster thriller and the hardline horror film — fall easily into familiar categories, obeying rules which have been fixed by repetition. This does not in itself diminish their capacity to excite; because if the director has sufficient control over his actors, cameraman, editor and composer, the oldest cliché in the book can still work perfectly. The thriller's conventional framework is by no means restrictive. It has been used frequently in the exploration of themes such as homosexuality and anti-semitism, which the front office would otherwise regard as taboo or financially disastrous. And even the most routine thriller is likely to contain something to catch the attention: a grotesque villain, a dynamic music score or perhaps an athletic chase sequence which unexpectedly starts the pulse racing long after boredom has set in.

The New Realism

By 1946, the screen gangster was virtually played out: Al Capone and his henchmen had died a thousand cinematic deaths and the world of the speakeasy had passed into oblivion. There was still the occasional revival — notably, Raoul Walsh's electrifying *White Heat* — but, as a general rule, the gangster was forced to give way to a new set of heroes and villains, including the spy, the safecracker, the detective and the private eye.

At about this time Hollywood discovered — or, more accurately, re-discovered — a novel approach to the thriller: the use of real locations and stories based on fact. Throughout the thirties and early forties, films set in New York, Havana, Rio de Janeiro or even farther afield had been defiantly filmed in downtown Los Angeles.

This so-called 'new realism' was largely the inspiration of Louis De Rochemont, a producer who, in 1935, had launched a series of newsreel-style, semi-documentary shorts under the collective title, *March of Time*. A characteristic of these shorts was the use of a stentorian narrator's voice — accurately parodied in the opening sequence of Orson Welles' *Citizen Kane* — which De Rochemont incorporated into his features to add to the impression of verisimilitude. His first full-length film, *The House on 92nd Street* (1946), about a secret agent who infiltrates a Nazi spy ring in New York, was based on a true story from the

Henry Hathaway's *The House on 92nd Street* (1946)

files of the FBI. The director, Henry Hathaway, who subsequently collaborated with De Rochemont on several features, uses his New York locations intelligently and, by filming the agent's *modus operandi* in detail, gives the film the look of a documentary.

Boomerang! (1947), produced by De Rochemont and directed by Elia Kazan, is a story, again based on fact, about the murder of an Episcopalian minister in a Connecticut town. The question of the accused man's guilt or innocence is never answered, but the claustrophobic atmosphere of a small town, shot in the studio. The film maintains a keen sense of actuality throughout, culminating in a galvanically filmed chase through the seedier areas of the city. Two years later, Dassin imported the semi-documentary technique into Britain for *Night and the City*, a slick American-style thriller set in the wrestling under-world, with a climactic chase filmed on London's waterfront.

Hathaway contributed two more excellent films to the genre: *Kiss of Death* (1947), a bleak New York-based thriller which marked the début of Richard Widmark as a sadistic killer with a disquieting laugh; and *Call Northside 777* (1948), which documents the efforts of a Chicago crime reporter (James

On pages 14–15
Henry Hathaway's *Kiss of Death* (1947). Richard Widmark and Victor Mature

Below
Jules Dassin's *The Naked City* (1948)

Stewart) to find a witness who can prove the innocence of an alleged murderer, convicted eleven years previously.

The vogue continued throughout the forties and into the early fifties with films like William Keighley's *The Street With No Name* (1948), Robert Siodmak's *Cry of the City* (1948), Elia Kazan's *Panic in the Streets* (1950) and Earl McEvoy's *The Frightened City* (1950). Even the traditionally studio-bound

Henry Hathaway's *Call Northside 777* (1948). James Stewart and Richard Conte

B-feature moved into the semi-documentary area with a series of undistinguished crime thrillers filmed mainly in Los Angeles, including Alfred Werker's *He Walked by Night* (1948) and Anthony Mann's *Side Street* (1949).

Of these later films, *Panic in the Streets* is perhaps the most interesting. It uses a fresh location – New Orleans – for its tense story of a health inspector turned detective (Richard Widmark,

Elia Kazan's *Panic in the Streets* (1950). Jack Palance

without the disquieting laugh) tracking down a killer who is believed to be carrying a most virulent form of plague.

In more recent films, the use of real locations rarely arouses much interest, but it is nonetheless interesting to note that William Friedkin's tough crime thriller *The French Connection* (1971), which makes admirable use of its wintertime New York setting, was produced by 20th Century-Fox, pioneers of the location thriller.

On pages 20–1
William Friedkin's *The French Connection* (1971). Gene Hackman

The Private Eye

The private-eye film, more precisely than any other genre, pins down the style and philosophy of Hollywood in the forties. So precisely, in fact, that contemporary variations on the theme almost always seem curiously displaced, as though they should really have been shot some twenty-five years earlier.

Howard Hawks's *The Big Sleep* (1946), adapted from the Raymond Chandler novel, is the archetypal 'shamus' thriller. Humphrey Bogart, who made his first foray into private-eye territory in John Huston's *The Maltese Falcon* (1941), played Philip Marlowe, and the screenwriters were novelist William Faulkner and two long-time Hawks associates, Leigh Brackett and Jules Furthman. None of them, the story goes, ever managed to figure out Chandler's convoluted plot.

Bogart, although the part seems to fit him like a glove, is actually miscast as Marlowe. He is too small, which gives rise to some acid dialogue in the opening sequences, and just a little too flippant, lisping well-turned wisecracks even when in extreme danger. But his lived-in look is perfect, and his violent denunciation of the smooth arch-villain, just before sending him to his death, catches the tone of the novel exactly.

Other Chandler adaptations, while adhering closely to the original plots, are less successful than Hawks's film. *Murder My Sweet* (1945, UK title *Farewell My Lovely*) is a near-miss.

Howard Hawks's *The Big Sleep* (1946). Humphrey Bogart

Edward Dmytryk's *Murder My Sweet* (1945, UK title *Farewell My Lovely*)
Dick Powell

24

Chandler himself felt that Dick Powell, in one of his first non-singing roles, came closer to his conception of Marlowe than any other actor who played the part. But Edward Dmytryk's direction, with its chiaroscuro lighting and weird special effects, veers towards the self-indulgent. The same is true of *Lady in the Lake* (1946), which Robert Montgomery both starred in and directed, using a 'subjective' camera technique. The audience sees only what Marlowe himself sees: driving a car, looking in a mirror, even getting punched on the nose. Although this is not without interest, it eventually becomes tiresome, and dissipates the suspense. *The Brasher Doubloon* (1947, UK title

Robert Montgomery's *Lady in the Lake* (1946). Robert Montgomery

John Brahm's *The Brasher Doubloon* (1947, UK title *The High Window*)

The High Window), weighed down by George Montgomery's wooden central performance and John Brahm's strictly routine direction, is the least distinguished of the forties Chandler adaptations.

A film based on an original screenplay by Chandler, George Marshall's *The Blue Dahlia* (1948), is a close variant on the Marlowe theme, although the plot actually concerns a former soldier suspected of killing his wife. There are some vintage Chandler lines in the script, but much of the plotting seems haphazard, and Alan Ladd's poker-faced performance is of little assistance.

26

George Marshall's *The Blue Dahlia* (1948). Alan Ladd

Jack Smight's *Harper* (1966, UK title *The Moving Target*). Pamela Tiffin and Robert Wagner

Apart from occasional appearances in lacklustre B-features and TV series, including some sanitized versions of the Marlowe stories, the private eye virtually disappeared from view during the fifties. In fact, he did not really surface again until 1966 with the release of Jack Smight's *Harper* (UK title *The Moving Target*), adapted by William Goldman from Ross Macdonald's sub-Chandler novel. Despite its contemporary setting, the film is a deliberately nostalgic exercise, even to the extent of including Lauren Bacall in the cast as an ageing lush. In true Chandler fashion, the plot is virtually impenetrable and the story moves along through a series of sharply written encounters between Harper, played in characteristic throwaway style by Paul Newman, and a nicely cast selection of Southern Californian freaks.

Gunn (1967), expanded by Blake Edwards from his long-running TV series, *Peter Gunn*, also has a nostalgic feel about it. The locale is Los Angeles and the plot line is appropriately confused, but the villain, as a concession to the new morality, is ultimately revealed as a drag queen. The climactic shoot-out in a plush apartment lined with mirrors borrows liberally from the hall of mirrors sequence in Orson Welles's *The Lady from Shanghai* (1948).

Blake Edwards's *Gunn* (1967). Craig Stevens

Buzz Kulik's *Warning Shot* (1966). David Janssen

Buzz Kulik's *Warning Shot* (1966), while not strictly speaking a private-eye film, duplicates the style almost exactly. The hero (David Janssen) is a suspended police officer who moves warily through a seedy Los Angeles milieu, encountering, among others, a suave and menacing company director, a precocious teenager and a wisecracking airline pilot. The year could as easily be 1946 as 1966.

If *Tony Rome* (1967) looks less obviously nostalgic, it is simply because the locale is Miami Beach. It has a familiar plot, involving the search for a diamond pin, and characters drawn

Gordon Douglas's *Tony Rome* (1967). Frank Sinatra

from stock. One American critic even thought it was an unacknowledged re-make of *The Big Sleep*. Rome, who borrows much of his style from Marlowe, is well played by Frank Sinatra, who perhaps comes closer than any other actor to catching Bogart's abrasive charm. There are some neat wisecracks in Richard L. Breen's screenplay – 'Nice ride,' says Sinatra, emerging from an elevator – and Gordon Douglas directs with a keen eye for both the elegance and garishness of the sun-soaked resort. A sequel, *Lady in Cement* (1968), is encumbered with a miscast Raquel Welch, an unconvincing homosexual milieu and inferior wisecracks by Marvin H. Albert and Jack Guss.

Ironically, the only direct adaptation made in the sixties from Chandler, Paul Bogart's *Marlowe* (1968, from the novel *The Little Sister*), is very much less successful than the Chandler imitations. James Garner is inadequate in the title role, Stirling Silliphant's screenplay is vapid and confused, while the appalling sets give the impression that it was made for a third-rate TV series.

In 1971, Gordon Parks's *Shaft* gave a new twist to the private-eye formula by setting its story in Harlem and casting black actor Richard Roundtree as the private eye. It is nevertheless very much a forties-based product, especially in the writing and playing of the minor parts: in particular, Willy (Drew Bundini Brown), one of the villain's henchmen, would have been perfectly at home swapping insults with Bogart. The author of the original novel and screenplay, Ernest Tidyman, admitted that he took many of his characters from the private-eye novels of Dashiell Hammett.

The phenomenal success of *Shaft*, one of the first Hollywood products to cash in on the rapidly-growing 'ethnic' market in America, inspired a sequel, *Shaft's Big Score* (1972), which

Gordon Parks's *Shaft's Big Score* (1972). Richard Roundtree

A British film, Stephen Frears's *Gumshoe* (1972), not only acknowledges the obligatory debt to the Hollywood private-eye films of the forties, but totally depends for its effect on the audience's knowledge of those films. The sad-eyed hero (Albert Finney) is a nightclub bingo-caller whose imagination has been dangerously coloured by the films of Humphrey Bogart and a collection of dog-eared Raymond Chandler and Dashiell Hammett novels. Setting himself up as a bona fide private eye, he quickly becomes embroiled in a lethal plot involving the smuggling of arms to South Africa. Andrew Lloyd-Webber's music parodies Max Steiner's score for *The Big Sleep*; a character called the Fat Man uncannily resembles Sydney Greenstreet; and Finney tends to conduct his conversations in the hard-boiled argot of the best private-eye films. It is an affectionate pastiche but in this case the genuine article is much superior.

The Spy

The spy in the cinema can be humorous, deadly, a threat to the nation, a joke or, latterly, a superhero with all the sophisticated technology of the twentieth century at his elegantly manicured fingertips. He changes with the times.

Immediately after World War II, Hollywood produced both semi-documentary reconstructions of espionage operations — such as *The House on 92nd Street* and *13 Rue Madeleine*, discussed earlier — and romantic adventure films in which the spy, while successfully protecting the security of the nation, takes time out to win the heart of an enigmatic young lady.

In Hitchcock's *Notorious* (1946), Cary Grant has little difficulty in bamboozling a Nazi spy ring in Rio de Janeiro — it involves hanging from a precipitously high building on Rio's spectacular waterfront — while falling in love with the daughter of a Nazi agent (Ingrid Bergman). Alan Ladd takes on the forces of evil in Irving Pichel's *OSS* (1946), making sure that his romantic aura is intact by walking off into the sunset with the cool and

Top
Alfred Hitchcock's *Notorious* (1946). Ingrid Bergman and Cary Grant

Bottom
Irving Pichel's *OSS* (1946). Alan Ladd

attractive, form of the espionage film emerged. It was a by-product of the fanciful imagination of Senator Joe McCarthy, who saw evidence of the Red Menace in the Hollywood dream factory, and succeeded in driving out such talented directors as Joseph Losey and Jules Dassin. His witch-hunt inspired a series of crude anti-Communist propaganda thrillers with sensational titles like *I Married a Communist* (1949) and *I Was a Communist for the FBI* (1952). The plots, whether fictional or based on fact, follow a similar pattern: machiavellian Reds, bent on undermining the American way of life, are ruthlessly defeated by the strong-arm tactics of the secret service.

Gordon Douglas's *I Was a Communist for the FBI* (1952). Frank Lovejoy

Samuel Fuller's *Pick-up on South Street* (1953).

The vogue lasted fitfully into the early sixties — with films like Andre De Toth's *Man on a String* (1960, UK title *Confessions of a Counter-Spy*), about a Russian-born Hollywood producer who works for Soviet agents in California — and, surprisingly, it produced at least one excellent thriller along the way: Samuel Fuller's *Pick-up on South Street* (1953). Adopting a semi-documentary format, the film has to do with a Communist plot to smuggle some microfilm out of America. Despite moments of hysteria and its political bias, the film is tense and convincing and, like most of Fuller's work, contains several bravura sequences. In one long take, an old woman is murdered — finally unseen by the camera — as she sits in bed, listening to her favourite record.

The more conventional spy thriller survived throughout the fifties and early sixties, although some of the romantic patina had been lost. George Seaton's *The Counterfeit Traitor* (1961),

George Seaton's *The Counterfeit Traitor* (1961). William Holden

for instance, is a big-budget action thriller, set in Occupied Europe, which finds time to investigate the conscience of its hero (William Holden). And a comparatively minor British thriller, Jack Lee's *Circle of Deception* (1960), questions the ethics of espionage techniques in the story of a secret agent (Bradford Dillman) whose life is broken by the callousness of his superiors.

In 1962, the spy film took a new and, financially, very profitable turn with the release of Terence Young's *Dr No*, adapted from the James Bond novel. Written and directed on the broadest

Terence Young's
Dr No (1962).
Sean Connery

series of adventure films in Britain during the fifties, realized they now had a potential goldmine on their hands, and stepped up the budgets for subsequent Bond adventures, on the philosophy that more is better. The villains, including the obese Goldfinger (Gerd Frobe) and the ubiquitous Blofeld (played by various actors) get increasingly outlandish; the puns roll off Bond's tongue with more polished ease: 'I think he got the point,' he comments, after killing someone with an arrow; and Ken Adam's sets, including a vast replica of the interior of Fort Knox and a missile launching-pad constructed inside a volcanic mountain, become progressively more fanciful. Unlike the books, which play the snobbery-with-violence game for real, the films take nothing seriously. The audience is invited to laugh at a supertechnology which has far outpaced its understanding; and, in a curious way, the films even help to make the nuclear age more bearable by sending up the most ludicrous aspects of international rivalry.

American studios, understandably annoyed at missing the filmic potential of the Bond books, were not slow to get in on the superspy act. Robert Vaughn and David McCallum are involved in the sporadically amusing *To Trap a Spy* (1965), directed by Don Medford as a pilot for the TV series, *The Man from UNCLE*. And Daniel Mann's *Our Man Flint* (1965) has James Coburn, one of the cool school of American actors, playing an American facsimile of Bond, complete with electronic bric-à-brac and an entourage of scantily-clad women. There are some pleasing inventions in the screenplay, including a cigarette lighter with fifty-eight different uses or, as Flint points out: 'Fifty-nine if you want to light a cigarette'. But the sequel, Gordon Douglas's *In Like Flint* (1967), is slack and confused, bringing the series to an abortive end. There is little of interest in the slapdash series of superspy escapades adapted from Donald Hamilton's Matt Helm books: *The Silencers*

Guy Hamilton's *Diamonds Are Forever* (1971). Sean Connery

Daniel Mann's *Our Man Flint* (1965). James Coburn

Phil Karlson's *The Silencers* (1966). Dean Martin

(1966), *Murderers' Row* (1966), *The Ambushers* (1967) and *The Wrecking Crew* (1968). The scripts are uninventive, the direction — by Phil Karlson and Henry Levin — computerized, and Dean Martin, as Helm, walks through them as though he really has something better to do with his time.

The French film industry also ventured into the area with a series of direly underwritten films involving an agent called OSS 117. The part was played variously by Kerwin Mathews, Frederick Stafford and John Gavin, none of whom could inject any life into the multi-national proceedings. However, some offbeat spy spoofs directed and written by Claude Chabrol, including *Le Tigre aime la chair fraîche* (1964) and *Marie Chantal contre le Docteur Kha* (1965), are visually imaginative and move at an enjoyably hectic pace.

In 1965, the Saltzman—Broccoli team launched a second series of spy films with *The Ipcress File*, based on the novel by Len Deighton. The hero, Harry Palmer (Michael Caine), does not inhabit a luxury penthouse, hop into bed with pneumatic blondes or overcome grotesque villains with a karate chop and a pun. He is a disgruntled civil servant, forced into espionage work after his release from prison. Yet, in their self-consciously downbeat way, the films create a world which is just as attractive as the one Bond moves in, and ultimately just as far removed from reality. Palmer's flat is decorated with the maximum of colour magazine chic, and Caine lends the character an undeniably glamorous anti-Establishment sheen.

The Ipcress File is the best of the series. It has an ingenious plot, a murder sequence intelligently borrowed from Fritz Lang's 1932 thriller, *The Testament of Dr Mabuse*, and some nicely quirky direction from Sidney J. Furie, who breaks up the cumbersome Cinemascope screen by photographing people and events from every conceivable angle. The second film, *Funeral in Berlin* (1966), has some good location work, but Guy Hamilton's direction is staid, and the over-elaborate plot is disastrous. *Billion-Dollar Brain* (1967) was entrusted to Ken

Sidney J. Furie's *The Ipcress File* (1965). Sue Lloyd and Michael Caine

Russell, whose firecracker talent proved woefully inadequate. A long, elaborate parody of the ice-battle sequence from Eisenstein's *Alexander Nevsky* misfires completely, and a scene in which a fanatical millionaire (Ed Begley) outlines his plans for taking over the world is embarrassingly overdone.

One of the few post-1960 films to catch something of the real spy's lifestyle is Martin Ritt's *The Spy Who Came in from the Cold* (1965), adapted from the best-selling novel by John Le Carré. Ritt's customary slow, measured pace is entirely in keeping with the film's fatalistic mood; Richard Burton's Leamas, a pawn in the Cold War game, carries exactly the right

49

Ken Russell's *Billion-Dollar Brain* (1967). Michael Caine

Martin Ritt's *The Spy Who Came in from the Cold* (1965). Richard Burton and Claire Bloom

Alfred Hitchcock's *Topaz* (1969)

air of disenchantment; and both director and star are abetted by Oswald Morris's superb black-and-white photography. Ritt's film and Sidney Lumet's *The Deadly Affair* are exceptions: a third thriller based on a Le Carré novel, Frank Pierson's *The Looking-Glass War* (1970), begins promisingly enough with a murder at a Scandinavian airport, but rapidly degenerates into an enervating adventure film in the James Bond mould.

Hitchcock contributed two new films to the spy series during the sixties: *Torn Curtain* (1966) and *Topaz* (1969), both of them miscalculated. There are isolated sequences of interest in *Topaz* — the opening chase, shot largely in reflection, and the murder of a Cuban informer — but the style of the film is rooted (this time fatally) in the forties. *Torn Curtain*, which has an inadequate script and some appalling sets, is only marginally better.

There is also one real curiosity which belongs, loosely, to the superspy genre: *Casino Royale* (1967), adapted from the

Casino Royale, directed by John Huston, Robert Parrish, Ken Hughes, Joe McGrath, Val Guest (1967). Orson Welles

James Bond novel, but produced by Charles K. Feldman, who bought the rights before the Saltzman–Broccoli team. It was obviously intended to send up the latter's Bond series – misguidedly, since the regular James Bond films parody themselves anyway – and its intentions were doubtless clearer to its five directors, John Huston, Robert Parrish, Ken Hughes, Joe McGrath and Val Guest, than to the public at large. Most of the film's stars, including Orson Welles, Peter Sellers and David Niven, play either James Bond, his namesake or one of his relatives, which further confuses the issue. But the film is by no means a total write-off: for instance, Ken Hughes's segment, involving a Mata Hari-style female spy (Anna Quayle), contains some well-executed visual gags and witty decor in the expressionistic style of *The Cabinet of Dr Caligari*. Elsewhere, George Raft puts in a pleasing brief appearance. Sitting disconsolately at a bar, he announces that his gun fires backwards. 'I've just shot myself,' he manages, before collapsing off his stool.

Thrillers with a Message

'If you excite your audience first,' Grahame Greene said, 'you can put over what you will of horror, suffering, truth.' Obeying his dictum, the cinema frequently uses the thriller format to examine themes which the front office would otherwise regard as unacceptable.

Politics is a case in point. Films with an overtly political theme have always been distrusted by the major studios for the understandable reason that most of them, like Franklin Schaffner's excellent *The Best Man* (1964), are disastrous box-office failures. But if the political pill is sugared — and the framework of the thriller can often provide an effective sweetener — directors can score their political points without alienating either the studios or the audience. It would be difficult, for instance, to envisage a more gripping thriller than John Frankenheimer's *The Manchurian Candidate* (1962), which builds up to a nerve-shattering climax in Madison Square Garden, or a more subtly-judged suspense film than the same director's *Seven Days in May* (1964), but both films also contain acute observations of the American political scene, and both issue timely caveats.

The Manchurian Candidate is about a Communist plot to use a brainwashed assassin (Laurence Harvey) to elevate a Communist puppet to the White House. Scripted by George Axelrod from Richard Condon's novel, the film is a more accurate and disturbing examination of the political power game than Otto Preminger's *Advise and Consent*, and its portraits of politicians, including a liberal senator and a miniature Joe McCarthy, always ring true. Directorially, it is superbly well organized. It opens in a Korean prisoner-of-war camp, where a group of American servicemen are being brainwashed into believing

John Frankenheimer's *The Manchurian Candidate* (1962). Laurence Harvey

John Frankenheimer's *Seven Days in May* (1964). Burt Lancaster, Fredric March and Kirk Douglas

they are attending a women's garden club meeting: the camera pans through 360 degrees, showing first the Korean interrogators, and then a group of middle-aged matrons. And Frankenheimer's obsession with technological gimmickry, particularly closed-circuit TVs, produces some appropriately dense compositions. In *Seven Days in May*, an Army colonel (Kirk Douglas) gradually realizes that one of his superiors (Burt Lancaster) is planning a military coup, and unilaterally sets about preventing it. Again the characterizations are convincing: the tired, anxious President (Fredric March), followed everywhere by a secret agent carrying the codes which could launch a nuclear war ; and the general, planning the coup because he genuinely believes that the President's decision to sign a nuclear treaty with the Russians is an invitation to disaster.

Henri-Georges Clouzot's *Le Salaire de la peur* (1953, *The Wages of Fear*) is remembered mainly as a high-tension account of a journey across rugged country by lorries loaded with explosive nitroglycerine. It is easy to overlook the fact that the first half of the film, taken at a leisurely pace to counterpoint the lorry sequences, is a portrait in depth of a small South American

Henri-Georges Clouzot's
Le Salaire de la peur
(1953, *The Wages of Fear*)

community whose political and economic life is totally dominated by American oil interests. Clouzot implies that the violent death of one of the drivers is preferable to the living death of the people in the poverty-stricken community.

Costa-Gavras's *Z* (1969) works simultaneously on two levels. It is as tense and tightly-sprung a thriller as some of the best examples of the genre, as well as being a savage full-scale attack on the totalitarian régime in Greece (the director's homeland) with a bitterly ironic epilogue. Similarly, the repressive police state is the real subject of Elio Petri's *Indagine su un cittadine al*

di sopra di ogno sospetto (1970, *Investigation of a Citizen Above Suspicion*). The ingenious story – about a police inspector who commits a murder, secure in the knowledge that he will never

Costa-Gavras's *Z* (1969)

Elio Petri's *Indagine su un cittadino al di sopra di ogno sospetto* (1970 *Investigation of a Citizen Above Suspicion*). Gian-Marie Volonte

be arrested – serves as a springboard for Petri to take a jaundiced look at the brutal interrogation methods of the Italian police and their neurotic hatred of the radical young.

The thriller framework also provides attractive cover for directors dealing with sociological and racial problems. Edward Dmytryk's *Crossfire* (1947) tackles the problem of anti-semitism in a story about a police investigation into the apparently motiveless murder of a middle-aged Jew. (In the original novel by film director Richard Brooks, the 'problem' was homosexuality, an unacceptable subject for Hollywood in the forties.) The film still works as a thriller, though the treatment of anti-semitism now seems innocuous and unnecessarily discreet, but there is no doubt that *Crossfire* marked an important breakthrough for the American cinema.

In *The World, the Flesh and the Devil* (1958), the writer-director, Ranald MacDougall, covers not only the race issue but

Edward Dmytryk's *Crossfire* (1947). Robert Ryan

Ranald MacDougall's *The World, the Flesh and the Devil* (1958). Harry Belafonte

also much wider problems of humanity in general. The plot involves three survivors of a nuclear war, one of them black (Harry Belafonte), who start their own private war on the photogenically deserted streets of New York. The film begins arrestingly, but quickly slides into glib generalization.

In Britain, the producer and director team of Michael Relph and Basil Dearden treated race prejudice far more successfully in *Sapphire* (1959). Janet Green's perceptive script, about the murder of a young black student, convincingly covers several areas of racial conflict. The same team subsequently moved

Basil Dearden's *Sapphire* (1959). Errol John and Nigel Patrick

into a more incendiary area with *Victim* (1961), about a respected lawyer (Dirk Bogarde), blackmailed for former homosexual associations. Despite an inevitable element of downpeddling — the lawyer is conveniently married to an attractive young woman (Sylvia Syms) — the film counters numerous misconceptions about homosexuals and courageously criticizes the archaic laws which, at the time, left homosexuals open to every conceivable form of blackmail.

Gordon Douglas's *The Detective* (1968), about the murder of a rich homosexual, is far more explicit in both its visuals and its language. In the opening scene, the detective (Frank Sinatra) coolly lists the details of the victim's mutilation, and, in an extended interrogation sequence, he puts his arm around a homosexual suspect as he questions him. Both as a thriller and as a plea for tolerance, the film is weakened by a superfluous subplot involving the detective's nymphomaniac wife (Lee Remick).

On pages 66–7
Gordon Douglas's *The Detective* (1968). Frank Sinatra

Below
Basil Dearden's *Victim* (1961). Sylvia Syms and Dirk Bogarde

Samuel Fuller's *The Crimson Kimono* (1959), which begins and ends as a tough urban thriller, takes time off in between to examine the problems of the Japanese community in Los Angeles. The account of Japanese mores is sympathetic, and the climactic chase in a Los Angeles street is an object lesson in

On the Waterfront (1954) actually works far better as a thriller than as an exposé of union racketeering. The real backgrounds – the bars, churches and bleak residential areas near the waterfront – and Marlon Brando's central performance as the inarticulate longshoreman give the film much of its force and drive. The union background is largely unconvincing, and the film's emphasis on individualism – Brando is beaten up by the corrupt racketeer and staggers, insisting on being unaided, along the waterfront to claim his right to work – seems oddly out of place.

Publicized as a courageous follow-up to *On the Waterfront*, Vincent Sherman's *The Garment Center* (1957, UK title *The Garment Jungle*), about corruption and mayhem in New York's garment district, cannot really stand comparison with Kazan's film. But it does have the advantages of an unusual setting and good performances by Lee J. Cobb as a factory owner and Richard Boone as a union-busting hoodlum. The film, begun by Robert Aldrich, who received no credit, was allegedly based on a true story. It must have come as a surprise to many people to learn that the garment industry was such a comprehensively nasty business.

Opposite
Elia Kazan's *On the Waterfront* (1954). Marlon Brando and Lee J. Cobb

On pages 72–3
Vincent Sherman's *The Garment Center* (1957, UK title: *The Garment Jungle*) Lee J. Cobb and Kerwin Matthews

The Chase

Whenever thriller scriptwriters run out of fresh ideas or novel twists, they can, and usually do, fall back on the genre's most popular stock device, the chase. It is the cinema's equivalent of the thriller novel's standard ploy, succinctly defined by Raymond Chandler in his book *The Simple Art of Murder*: 'When in doubt, have a man come through the door with a gun in his hand.' Most thrillers manage to find room for at least one variation on the chase. Perhaps the hero will be shadowed by a mysterious shifty-eyed stranger; or someone will leap into a taxi with the command, 'Follow that car!'; or the villain, after successfully eluding the police, will run out of places to hide and fall off the top of the highest building in town. But while the chase is a basic common denominator of the thriller, and has been relentlessly pressed into service by almost every grade-B movie ever made, it has also provided some of the genre's most accomplished writers and directors with the basis of their plots.

The chase, for instance, is the *sine qua non* of Hitchcock's *North by Northwest* (1959), based on an original screenplay by Ernest Lehman. Cary Grant, as the adman suspected of being a spy, spends virtually the entire film pursued by, and occasionally in pursuit of, a ring of evil spies. The locale shifts from the United Nations building to a country estate, then to Grand Central

Station, a train, the corn fields outside Chicago and, finally and most spectacularly, to Mount Rushmore in South Dakota.

The film's plot bears a very close resemblance to *The Thirty-Nine Steps,* originally filmed by Hitchcock in 1935 and re-made by Ralph Thomas in 1959. Once again, an innocent man (Robert Donat in the original, and Kenneth More in the later version) is pursued by both police and villains. Thomas's adaptation of John Buchan's novel owes less to the book than to Hitchcock's film, from which it borrows most of its set pieces, including the music-hall climax, and the humorous tone.

Two films directed in Britain by Stanley Donen, *Charade* (1963) and *Arabesque* (1966), also borrow extensively from

On pages 76–7
Stanley Donen's *Charade* (1963) George Kennedy and Cary Grant

Below
Ralph Thomas's *The Thirty-Nine Steps* (1959). Taina Elg and Kenneth More

Hitchcock, especially from *North by Northwest*. In *Charade*, scripted by Peter Stone, Cary Grant and Audrey Hepburn pursue both each other and a group of bizarre villains around Mégève and the more fashionable *arrondissements* of Paris. The jokier elements in the plot occasionally dissipate the tension (*North by Northwest*, on the other hand, strikes a fine balance between humour and thrills) but it finishes in fine style with two extended chases. In the first, a bemused Audrey Hepburn is chased through the Metro by Grant, whom she mistakenly

Stanley Donen's *Arabesque* (1966). Sophia Loren and Gregory Peck

believes to be the murderer: then, after revealing his true identity, Grant frantically pursues the real murderer (Walter Matthau) through the theatre at the Palais Royale.

Arabesque has a similar theme and an equally chic setting. Another professional man (Gregory Peck) becomes involved with a beautiful and enigmatic woman (Sophia Loren) and finds himself the target of a group of Middle Eastern assassins. In this case, however, Donen's flashy technique is unable to disguise weaknesses in the plot and the banality of much of the

pseudo-sophisticated dialogue (Peter Stone, under the *nom de plume* of Pierre Marton, also contributed to this screenplay). But the film does contain two excellent chases: a pursuit around Regent's Park Zoo, with birds shrieking wildly in the background, and a climactic chase involving a helicopter and a combine harvester.

Philippe De Broca's *L'Homme de Rio* (1963, *That Man from Rio*) takes the mock-chase thriller to its logical conclusion. The athletic star (Jean-Paul Belmondo) is required to brave vertigo on the top of half-constructed buildings in Brasilia, to leap from planes and fall into the jaws of a crocodile, and to participate in the most shattering bar-room brawl ever put on celluloid. The tone of the film is determinedly flippant, and it is directed, written and acted with *élan*.

In the forties and early fifties, the chase was a more serious affair. There is nothing flippant, for instance, about the gritty chases in either of Jules Dassin's semi-documentary thrillers, *Naked City* and *Night and the City*. Dick Powell, after his success

Philippe De Broca's *L'Homme de Rio* (1963, *That Man from Rio*). Jean-Paul Belmondo

Edward Dmytryk's *Cornered* (1946). Dick Powell

in *Farewell My Lovely*, made two tough 'manhunt' thrillers: in Edward Dmytryk's *Cornered* (1946), he plays a former Canadian air ace who travels through France, Switzerland and Argentina

Robert Stevensons' *To the Ends of the Earth* (1948). Dick Powell

searching for the Nazis who killed his wife; and in Robert
Stevenson's *To the Ends of the Earth* (1948), he is an American
agent tracking dope-smugglers half-way around the world.

Don Siegel's *The Big Steal* (1949) is a chase from start to
finish: the locale is South America, and the participants are
Robert Mitchum as the pursued, and William Bendix as the
pursuer. Because of Mitchum's unavailability at the start of
shooting, the film was made, very obviously, at different times
of the year, which lends an almost surreal quality to the pursuit.
In Rudolf Maté's *D.O.A.* (1949), Edmond O'Brien, the star, was

Don Siegel's *The Big Steal* (1949). Robert Mitchum and Jane Greer

Yates's handling of the *Robbery* chase — slinging cameras underneath, inside and on top of cars — which earned him the *Bullitt* assignment.

The car chase can be jokey: the Bond film *Diamonds are Forever* (1971), directed by Guy Hamilton, contains a spectacular chase around the streets of Las Vegas, which would not have been out of place in a Mack Sennett comedy. The high

Henri Verneuil's *Le Cassé* (1971, *The Burglars*). Omar Sharif

92

Guy Hamilton's *Diamonds Are Forever* (1971)

point of Henri Verneuil's *Le Cassé* (1971, *The Burglars*) is an amusingly hair-raising chase between a car and the athletic Jean-Paul Belmondo who leaps between trams, cars and buses in his attempts to avoid capture. And the climactic chase in Richard Brooks's *Dollars* (1972, UK title *The Heist*) involves cars, trains and lorries.

More frequently, though, it is a deadly affair. In Richard Fleischer's *The Last Run* (1971) an ageing gangster (George C. Scott), tempted out of retirement, drives furiously down dusty mountain roads, proving that his former ability has not entirely deserted him. Doug Hickox's *Sitting Target* (1972) culminates

On pages 94–5
Richard Brooks's *Dollars* (1972, UK title *The Heist*). Warren Beatty and Goldie Hawn

Steven Spielberg's *Duel* (1972). Dennis Weaver

New York, substitutes motor-bikes for cars. And in Steven Spielberg's *Duel* (1972) a travelling saleman (Dennis Weaver) conducts a running battle in his car with a curiously malicious lorry-driver.

On pages 98–9
William Friedkin's *The French Connection* (1971)

But the most riveting car chase takes place in William Friedkin's *The French Connection* (1971), a semi-documentary story of a narcotics shake-down made by *Bullitt*'s producer, Philip D'Antoni. The chase is perfectly integrated into the plot — which is not always true of chases — and the participants are a ruthless cop (Gene Hackman) in a borrowed car, and an equally ruthless dope-smuggler, who is trapped in a subway train on the elevated sector of the track in Brooklyn. Friedkin's marvellously fluid camera shows the car and the train in long-shot, then moves in close for a driver's eye view of the chase as the car narrowly avoids bridges, pedestrians and a pram.

The *Psycho* Syndrome

Alfred Hitchcock's *Psycho* (1960), one of the most influential and profitable of all post-war thrillers, was savagely treated by most British and American critics on its initial release. It was the director's choice of subject-matter – the use of mental illness as the mainspring of the plot – which disturbed them rather than the way he manipulated his audience in achieving his horrific effects. The ethics of the film are, perhaps, open to doubt, but there is no question that it is an insidiously clever piece of film-making.

It begins as a conventional 'heist' thriller. The credit titles, rolling over a high-angle shot of a large American city, inform us that it is 2 : 43 on a Friday in Phoenix, Arizona. An attractive young woman (Janet Leigh) steals some money from her employers and drives off into the night. She is stopped, briefly, by an ominous-looking cop – an excellent red herring – runs into some bad weather and pulls up at a deserted motel run by the disturbed, but apparently harmless, Norman Bates (Anthony Perkins). The audience has a character to identify with – she is a thief, but villains are often more sympathetic than heroes – and the question posed by the film seems simple : will she get away with the money? But Hitchcock is playing a totally different game. The girl takes a shower in her motel room and is savagely murdered – apparently by Bates's mother. The film

abruptly changes direction, completely disturbing the audience's preconceptions. And an insurance investigator (Martin Balsam), the second character to engage the audience's sympathy, is also killed.

The murders are brilliantly shot and edited. The shower sequence is horrifying and explicit, though the director cuts away before the knife enters the flesh. The investigator is murdered after climbing a long flight of stairs in the decaying mansion adjoining the motel. The camera follows him up the stairs then switches to an unnerving high-angle shot as he reaches the top, to be met by the old woman rushing out of her bedroom with a knife held high in the air. Piercing violins on the soundtrack — the music is by Hitchcock's long-time associate, Bernard Herrman — help to fray the nerves. And the climactic revelation — that Bates and his 'mother' are one and the same person — is also given maximum impact.

A familiar logic guarantees that most thrillers, while generating tension, simultaneously console the audience. The *Psycho* 'school' borrows its rules from the horror genre and deliberately sets out to disturb and disorientate the audience. Henri-Georges Clouzot's *Les Diaboliques* (1955) belongs in the same category as *Psycho* — but the latter's influence has been much more widely felt.

It quickly inspired a series of lacklustre imitations from the British Hammer studios, which had previously specialized in Dracula and Frankenstein. The titles, including *Maniac* (1962), *Paranoiac* (1963) and *Fanatic* (1964), make both their intentions and their source abundantly clear, but the films play far less subtly than *Psycho* on the audience's preconceptions and sense of identification. Their supposedly horrific effects are rarely achieved with any finesse. The characters are mere cyphers,

Alfred Hitchcock's *Psycho* (1960). Anthony Perkins

Michael Carreras's *Maniac* (1962). Kerwin Matthews

mill. Greene's edgy direction, including some exceptionally good hand-held work, keeps the temperature high.

In America, William Castle, a specialist in cheap second-features, directed an enervating series of *Psycho*-based films — including *Straitjacket* (1963) — most of them played, ineffectively, for laughs. But several other directors co-opted the *Psycho* motif with more imaginative, if not necessarily less sensational, results. A prime example is *Peeping Tom*, made in 1959 by Michael Powell, a director who had collaborated with Emeric Pressburger in writing, producing and directing some of the most distinguished British films of the forties, including *A Matter of Life and Death* (1946, US title *Stairway to Heaven*) and *The Red Shoes* (1948). Like *Psycho*, *Peeping Tom* was savaged by the critics when it first appeared. It is not difficult to see why: the central character (Carl Boehm) is an emotional cripple who films young girls as he murders them with the tripod of his camera, forcing them to watch themselves die in a mirror. He then projects the films in his studio, to the accompaniment of tapes of himself, as a child, screaming while being tortured by his father.

Despite some evidence of a low budget in the quality of the sets, the entire film is shot with an appropriately bizarre brilliance, making full expressionistic use of sound and films-within-films. Key scenes are played out against a background of the cinema screen or in the light shining from the projector. In the final sequence, the police arrive at the photographer's house — a moment he is fully prepared for. Switching on all the tapes and cameras, he rushes across the room, filming himself from every angle, and impales himself on the tripod. The screen goes dark, the projector stops, and all the tapes finish but one: a child's voice — his own — says plaintively, 'Daddy, hold my hand.' The film's writer, Leo Marks, devised an equally distasteful plot for

On pages 108–9
Michael Powell's *Peeping Tom* (1959). Carl Boehm and Anna Massey

Roy Boulting's *Twisted Nerve* (1968). But without the saving grace of Powell's brilliant technique, the film seems merely repellent.

Roman Polanski re-worked the *Psycho* formula in his British-made *Repulsion* (1965), about a sexually repressed young woman (Catherine Deneuve) who turns into a homicidal maniac. More disquieting than the actual murders is Polanski's imagery. A rabbit lies decomposing on the kitchen table, a tangible reflection of the girl's paranoia; and as she walks

Georges Franju's *Les Yeux sans visage* (1959, *Eyes Without a Face*). Edith Scob

down a corridor, hands reach out of the walls attempting to molest her.

Georges Franju's *Lex Yeux sans visage* (1959, *Eyes Without a Face*), adapted from a novel by Boileau and Narcejac, authors of *Les Diaboliques*, actually anticipated *Psycho* by several months. The plot is straightforward horror material. A mad doctor, responsible for disfiguring his daughter's face in a car accident, kidnaps young girls and vainly attempts to graft their skin on to hers. Finally, his own face is ripped off by the dogs he keeps in his cellar for experimental purposes. His daughter wanders off, Ophelia-like, into the dark. Franju, known previously for his documentaries, directs the film with a rigid, formal elegance. The pace is slow, and the horror is suggested rather than shown : the doctor puts a victim on the operating table and pencil-marks her face in the places where he is going to insert the knife. The tension between the full-blooded horror of the plot and the film's ice-cold surface (the sharp black-and-white photography is by Eugen Shufftan) freezes the blood.

In 1962 the *Psycho*-style film went off on a slightly different tangent with the release of Robert Aldrich's *Whatever Happened to Baby Jane?* Two ageing sisters play out a deadly, maniacal game in their decaying Hollywood mansion. Jane (Bette Davis), a former child star, is insanely jealous of Blanche (Joan Crawford), who is now a cripple, drunkenly torments her, and finally tries to kill her. There is a sting in the tail : Blanche admits that she was responsible for the car accident which crippled her. Jane, who was drunk during the accident, had always thought herself responsible for it.

A similar formula was used for a sequel, *Hush, Hush Sweet Charlotte* (1964), also directed by Aldrich. Charlotte (Bette Davis), who lives in the crumbling mansion where her lover was murdered with a meat-cleaver, is reunited with her long-lost sister (Olivia De Havilland) who, together with her lover (Joseph Cotten), sets about terrifying her.

Curiously, both these Grand Guignol works are suffused with

Robert Aldrich's *Whatever Happened to Baby Jane?* (1962). Bette Davis

Robert Aldrich's *Hush, Hush Sweet Charlotte* (1964). Bette Davis

a strange kind of tenderness, a sense of innocence lost. Both begin with long pre-credit sequences set some thirty years before the main action. In *Hush, Hush Sweet Charlotte*, the scene is a ball in an elegant Southern mansion, with chandeliers tinkling in the warm evening breeze; in *Whatever Happened to Baby Jane?*, it is a dazzling Hollywood première, where everyone is young and enthusiastic, and Los Angeles is not yet impersonal and tawdry.

The series continued fitfully with films like Bernard Girard's *Whoever Slew Auntie Roo?* (1969), but only Curtis Harrington's excellent *Whatever Became of Aunt Helen?* (1972), with Debbie Reynolds as an ageing dance teacher, catches the style of the two Aldrich films.

Samuel Fuller's *Shock Corridor* (1963). Peter Breck

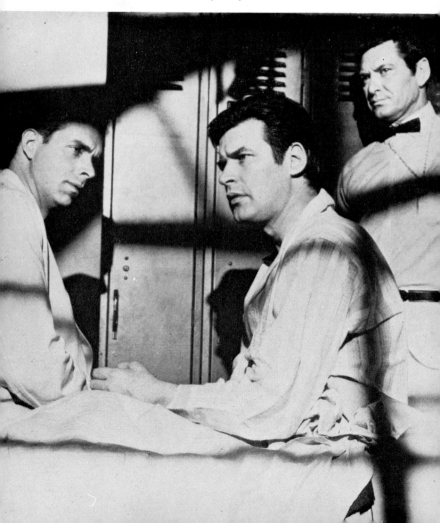

The world of madness proved irresistibly attractive to Samuel Fuller, a director whose gift for powerful visuals and sensational subject-matter is sometimes mistaken for corrosive genius. *Shock Corridor*, made in 1963 and banned for many years by the British Board of Film Censors, is about a reporter (Peter Breck), desperate to win the Pulitzer Prize for journalism, who enters a lunatic asylum to solve a murder case and finishes up a patient. As with most of Fuller's work, the film combines moments of power and originality – a black patient, believing he is a member of the Ku Klux Klan, delivers furious racist tirades – with a dialogue of ludicrous pretentiousness. The wooden reporter has a tendency to drop inapposite literary references into his otherwise monosyllabic speech.

Two films which fit a little uneasily into the *Psycho* category are *The Boston Strangler* (1968) and *10 Rillington Place* (1971), both based on real-life murder cases and both directed by Richard Fleischer. The former, a totally unsensational reconstruction of the Boston murders, is by far the more successful of the two. After recording the painstaking police investigation into the murders, the film ends with a virtuoso sequence in which the strangler, played with surprising restraint by Tony Curtis, gradually breaks down as he recognizes the dual nature of his personality. *10 Rillington Place*, based on the Christie murders in Notting Hill Gate, London, lacks the same conviction. Richard Attenborough, as Christie, struggles valiantly against miscasting, and Clive Exton's script takes unnecessary liberties with the known facts. In *No Way to Treat a Lady* (1968) Jack Smight uses the Boston murders as the basis for a black comedy, with Rod Steiger, in disguises ranging from a camp hairdresser to a priest, as the mass-murderer.

Peter Bogdanovitch's *Targets* (1968), while not based on any specific incident, variously reflects and anticipates several real-life murders. An apparently well-balanced Army veteran, living

On pages 116–17
Richard Fleischer's *The Boston Strangler* (1968). Tony Curtis

with his wife at his parents' house, shoots his entire family and drives out to an oil refinery near the Sunset Strip, where he arbitrarily picks off victims on the freeway. Implicit in the story is a criticism of American gun laws which allow any citizen to buy as many guns and as much ammunition as he wants, but there is no direct attempt to explain the young man's actions.

The film's sub-plot involves a young film director (Bogdanovitch himself) who is attempting to persuade an ageing horror star (Boris Karloff) to appear in his new film, despite the actor's conviction that he should have retired long ago. In the final section of the film, the two stories are successfully interwoven. The sniper picks off his last victims at a drive-in cinema where the actor's latest film is being premièred. And it is the actor himself who finally puts an end to it. 'So that's what I was afraid of,' he says, as the young man lies whimpering on the ground.

Opposite
Jack Smight's *No Way to Treat a Lady* (1968). Rod Steiger
Below
Peter Bogdanovitch's *Targets* (1968). Tim O'Kelly

The Heist

Before regulations were unofficially relaxed in the late sixties, the forces of censorship and assorted legions of decency ensured that crime, at least in the movies, did not pay. It was essential that the bank robber, the safecracker and the jewel thief were caught, and their ill-gotten gains returned to their rightful owners. The question put to the audience was not whether the thieves would get away with it, but how and when they would be trapped — making the director's job of maintaining tension that much more difficult.

In one of the best of all heist thrillers, John Huston's *The Asphalt Jungle* (1950), the actual robbery, of a jewelry store, is thrown away in a ten-minute sequence in the middle of the picture. What makes the film exceptional is the range and depth of the characterization: the polite jewel thief with an eye for young girls; the strong-arm man (Sterling Hayden) who dreams of returning to his home in the country and dies in the process; the hunchbacked lunchroom operator (James Whitmore); and the philandering lawyer (Louis Calhern) who bankrolls the robbery from non-existent funds. The thieves, although they fail, are as professional, perhaps as ethical, as members of 'straight' society. 'Crime,' as the lawyer says, 'is merely a left-handed form of human endeavour.'

The Asphalt Jungle, based on a novel by W.R. Burnett, was

Barry Pollack's *Cool Breeze* (1972). Raymond St Jacques and Stack Pierce

On pages 122–3
Jules Dassin's *Du Rififi chez les hommes* (1954, *Rififi*)

re-made in 1972 as *Cool Breeze*, with black actors taking over all the leading roles. Unfortunately, Barry Pollack, who directed and wrote, reduces the thieves to mere stereotypes – the super-cool hero, the muscle-bound strong-arm man – and turns the robbery into a mistimed joke, with the thieves wearing rubber masks of Richard Nixon, Spiro Agnew and George Wallace.

Another classic heist thriller, *Du Rififi chez les hommes* (*Rififi*, 1954), directed in France by American expatriate Jules

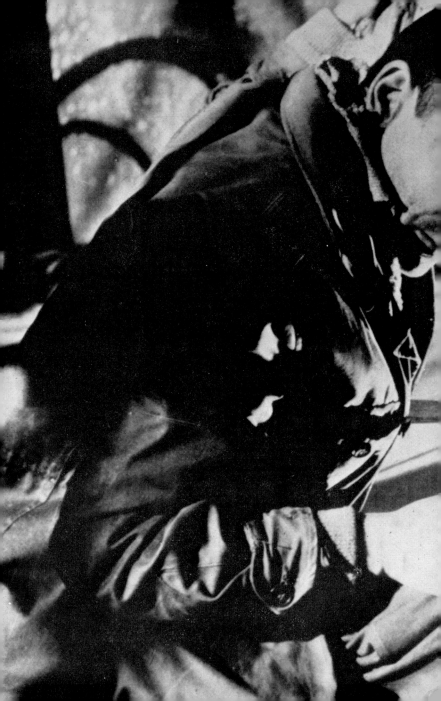

Dassin, is also about the robbery of a jewelry store. In this case the robbery itself is the outstanding sequence. It lasts for half an hour and is played entirely without dialogue — the use of incidental sounds is minimal — making its impact extraordinarily powerful. The characterization, too, is unusually sharp. In the final sequence, the leader of the gang (Jean Servais), who suffers from a tubercular condition, drives crazily through Paris after being reunited with his son. His dream ends as surely, and pathetically, as Hayden's in *The Asphalt Jungle*.

Jewels and jewelry stores are favourite targets of robbers in the

Jules Dassin's *Topkapi* (1964)

cinema. Dassin himself re-worked his *Rififi* theme in *Topkapi* (1964), about a gang of ill-assorted thieves who steal a gem-encrusted diamond from a museum in Istanbul. The robbery sequence is taut — the thieves have to be lowered from the roof, because the floor of the museum is wired for sound — but the rest of the film is a genial Ealing-style comedy, with a bumbling Peter Ustinov providing most of the laughs.

Ronald Neame's *Gambit* (1966) is another 'caper' picture. A likeable con-man (Michael Caine) conceives an ingenious plan for stealing a priceless *objet d'art* from a Middle Eastern

Peter Ustinov in *Topkapi*

Peter Yates's *The Hot Rock* (1972, U K title *How to Steal a Diamond in Four Uneasy Lessons*). George Segal

millionaire (Herbert Lom), enlisting the help of a recalcitrant nightclub dancer (Shirley MacLaine). Everything goes according to plan – because it is happening only in Caine's imagination. In reality, everything goes disastrously wrong : the millionaire, a misanthropic recluse in Caine's version of the theft, turns out to be a sophisticated man-about-town. The excellent plot twists were provided by Alvin Sargent and Jack Davies.

Peter Yates's equally flippant *The Hot Rock* (1972, U K title *How to Steal a Diamond in Four Uneasy Lessons*) takes advantage of the new moral freedom by allowing its protagonists to get away with it. The robbery is very funny – one of the gang

Zero Mostel in *The Hot Rock*

Bryan Forbes's *Deadfall* (1968). Michael Caine

(George Segal) gets trapped in the glass case which is protecting the diamond — and all the performances, particularly Zero Mostel's cameo of a 'bent' lawyer, help to create a pleasantly relaxed mood. At the end of the film, one of the thieves (Robert Redford), having finally got his hands on the gem, walks joyously down a New York street, to the accompaniment of a witty score by Quincy Jones.

Bryan Forbes's *Deadfall* (1968), another jewel robbery piece, is written and directed in a very different vein. The thieves in this case are an ambitious young cat-burglar (Michael Caine) and an older cracksman (Eric Portman), a homosexual who has lost

129

his self-respect. The robbery sequence is long and silent, but less tense than *Rififi*'s because the feats performed by Caine look impossible, and the whole sequence is tiresomely cross-cut with a classical concert. The film's more serious overtones are lost in the glamorous Majorca settings.

Henri Verneuil's *Le Clan des Siciliens* (1969, *The Sicilian Clan*) is a much bigger affair. The thieves (led by Jean Gabin and Alain Delon) hijack an aeroplane and force it to land on a half-completed freeway near New York to get their hands on its multi-million cargo of jewelry. In addition to this exceptional set piece, the film contains some inventive escape sequences. To get out of a police van, Delon cuts a hole in the floor with a circular saw; and later, caught in bed with a prostitute, he swings out of the window and across the rooftops of Paris with the panache of a latter-day Douglas Fairbanks.

The bank robbery is an equally popular theme, and just as adaptable. Like the jewel robbery, it is frequently played for laughs. Basil Dearden's *The League of Gentlemen* (1960), about a gang of unusually well-heeled thieves who rob a London bank, is essentially a civilized comedy, though the robbery sequence — the thieves set off smoke bombs and don gas masks — is quite tense. Bernard Girard's underrated *Dead-Heat on a Merry-Go-Round* (1967) is about the robbery of a bank at Los Angeles International Airport, planned to coincide with the visit of the Russian premier; it has a wittily ironic script (by Girard himself) and a beguiling performance by James Coburn as the con-man who masterminds the operation.

The joke can sometimes go too far. With its modish use of split-screens, leisurely pace and glamorous stars (Steve McQueen and Faye Dunaway), Norman Jewison's *The Thomas Crown Affair* (1968), about a millionaire who robs a

Norman Jewison's *The Thomas Crown Affair* (1968). Steve McQueen

131

Basil Dearden's *The League of Gentlemen* (1960)

bank for kicks, looks more like a commercial for after-dinner mints than a thriller. And Richard Brooks's *Dollars* (UK title: *The Heist*), set in Hamburg, is also dangerously cool. Only the actual robbery — carried out under a swivelling electronic eye — succeeds in raising the temperature.

On a more serious level, Richard Fleischer's *Violent Saturday* (1955) is a taut and detailed account of a bank robbery in a small mining town, all the more effective because it observes the unities of time and place. The small-time thieves (including Richard Egan, Victor Mature and the young Lee Marvin) are

Richard Fleischer's *Violent Saturday* (1955). J. Carrol Naish and Lee Marvin

Opposite
Lewis Milestone's *Ocean's 11* (1960). Frank Sinatra

well fleshed out, and the atmosphere of the tightly-knit community is sympathetically recorded.

The casino, of course, makes a more glamorous target for the screen thief. In Lewis Milestone's *Ocean's 11* (1960), Danny Ocean (Frank Sinatra) recruits eleven members of his wartime

commando battalion to carry out a series of raids on Las Vegas casinos. Unhappily, Saul Bass's brash credit titles are more interesting than the film, but the final tracking shot is haunting: after watching their money go up in flames, the thieves walk sadly and silently away from a Las Vegas church.

Henry Hathaway's *Seven Thieves* (1960) is a more imaginative variation on the casino theme. An ageing criminal (Edward G. Robinson) decides to pull off one last coup before retiring: raiding the casino in Cannes. He enlists the grudging assistance of a younger man (Rod Steiger) — his son, though we only learn this in the final sequence. Hathaway organizes the operation superbly: he even brings off such a hoary old cliché as the thief who loses his nerve climbing along a balcony. At the end of the film, the old man dies of a heart attack, believing that the robbery has been a complete success. There is a final ironic twist: the money is numbered, and the thieves therefore have to return it to the casino.

Henri Verneuil's *Melodie en sous-sol* (1962, UK title *The Big Snatch*; US title *Any Number Can Win*) has a similar plot. The thieves are an ageing cracksman (Jean Gabin) and his self-confident assistant (Alain Delon), and their target, again, is the Cannes casino. At the end of the film, as the police move in, the thieves throw the suitcases containing the money into a swimming pool. They sit placidly round the edge of the pool as the water erodes the suitcases and the money drifts to the surface.

Henry Hathaway's *Seven Thieves* (1960). Edward G. Robinson, Joan Collins, Rod Steiger

Sidney Lumet's *The Anderson Tapes* (1971) is a heist thriller for the seventies. A master criminal (Sean Connery), recently released from jail, plans to rob an entire apartment block on New York's fashionable East Side. But every move made by himself and his associates is methodically filmed and taped by assorted detectives and Government agents, and the details fed into computers. When they die after failing to bring off the robbery, their files are perfunctorily destroyed.

Opposite
Henri Verneuil's *Melodie en sous-sol* (1962, UK title *The Big Snatch*; US title *Any Number Can Win*). Alain Delon

Sidney Lumet's *The Anderson Tapes* (1971). Sean Connery

Other Parts of the Forest

'Off the hump of Brazil I saw an ocean so black . . . the sea was made of sharks and more sharks still . . . the beasts took to eating each other . . . there wasn't one that survived.' The lines are from Orson Welles's *The Lady from Shanghai* (1948), which takes a formula plot — about a sailor (played by Welles himself) trapped into a charge of murder by an impotent lawyer (Everett Sloane) and his predatory wife (Rita Hayworth) — and turns it into a poetic vision of evil. With the exception of the sailor, all the characters are consumed by ambition and greed; as with the sharks, not one survives.

The entire film has a dream-like, hallucinatory quality. A luxurious yacht drifts lazily through tropical waters; the sailor's trial becomes an absurd nightmare; and a confrontation takes place in a San Francisco aquarium, with magnified fish pouting obscenely in the background. Fittingly, the nightmare ends in a deserted fairground, where the lawyer and his wife kill each other in a hall of distorting mirrors. Welles uses the conventions of the thriller as a kind of cinematic short-hand: an easily accessible means to a surrealistic end.

He returned to Hollywood in 1958 to make *Touch of Evil*, which involves a narcotics investigator (Charlton Heston), honeymooning in a Mexican border-town, who exposes a corrupt American cop, Quinlan (Welles), and his sinister

Orson Welles's *The Lady from Shanghai* (1948). Orson Welles

associates. Once again, Welles's richly imaginative direction turns it into a nightmare vision: the camera tracks fluidly round the morally dank town (constructed on the Universal lot in Hollywood); and most of the action — at least three separate stories are interwoven — takes place in semi-darkness. Welles himself is magnificent as the tragic, self-destructive Quinlan.

Robert Aldrich's *Kiss Me Deadly* (1955) is a nightmare from beginning to end. Adapted — or, more accurately, wrenched from — Mickey Spillane's thick-ear novel of the same name, the film is totally nihilistic, from its conception of the emotionally bleak hero, private eye Mike Hammer (Ralph Meeker), to the credit titles which, appropriately, roll on backwards. Hammer

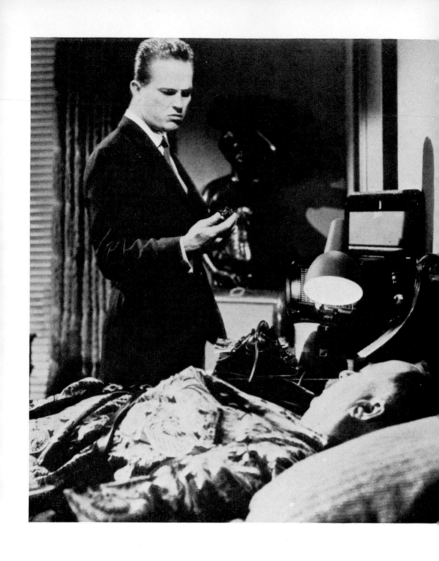

Robert Aldrich's *Kiss Me Deadly* (1955). Ralph Meeker

picks up a frightened girl on the highway and blunders into a situation which is beyond his meagre comprehension. Both he and the equally unsympathetic villains are trying to get their hands on a mysterious black box containing an undefined but instantly combustible weapon which, in the final moments, explodes as Hammer and his girlfriend wander uncomprehendingly into the sea. The film is permeated by an air of corruption and hardcore nastiness, accentuated by the lighting. Interrogating a failed opera singer, Hammer picks up a record: 'I'd say this was a priceless item,' he says coolly, and breaks it in two. A perfectly ordinary household in which Hammer conducts an abortive interview is inexplicably racked by fear.

If *Kiss Me Deadly*, with its grotesquely stylized violence, takes the B-feature thriller to its logical conclusion, Jean-Luc Godard takes it to its illogical conclusion. Most of his early films are based on thriller novels and use thriller techniques, but their purpose is not to excite. There is no attempt at surface naturalism: Michel (Jean-Paul Belmondo), the hero of Godard's first film *A bout de souffle* (1959, *Breathless*), dies violently in a Paris street, but the passers-by fail to notice him as he staggers crazily from side to side. The gangsters in *Bande à part* (1964, UK title *The Outsiders*; US title *Band of Outsiders*) borrow their gestures and their language from B-features, and they die in wild parodies of a screen gangster's death-throes. *Pierrot le Fou* (1965), adapted from a straightforward American thriller by Lionel White, is packed even more densely with filmic quotes, literary allusions, political discussion. Ferdinand (Jean-Paul Belmondo) occasionally talks direct to the audience and, at the end of the film, he commits suicide by fixing an absurd amount of dynamite to his head. American director Sam Fuller puts in a brief appearance early on in this existential thriller, expounding

On pages 144–5
Jean-Luc Godard's *A bout de souffle* (1959). Jean-Paul Belmondo

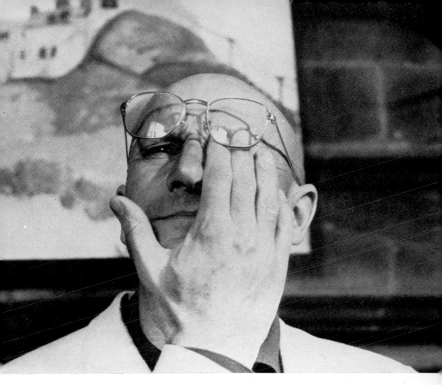

Roman Polanski's *Cul-de-sac* (1966). Donald Pleasance

his view that the cinema is a battleground, 'or in one word: emotion'.

'A battleground' adequately describes René Clément's *Les Félins* (1964, UK title *The Love Cage*; US title *Joy House*). After escaping death by drowning, by high-speed car and by express train in the space of five minutes, a professional cardsharp (Alain Delon), on the run from American hoodlums, is caught between Lola Albright and Jane Fonda in a lethal *ménage à trois*. He tries to play one off against the other, only to find that there is no escape.

After *Repulsion* Roman Polanski made the surrealistic thriller *Cul-de-sac* (1966), a Pinteresque story about two gangsters

On pages 148–9
René Clément's *Les Félins* (1964, UK title *The Love Cage*; US title *Joy House*). Alain Delon

Arthur Penn's *Mickey One* (1965) has all the superficial qualities of a suspense thriller. Mickey, a minor nightclub comedian, is pursued through the junk-yards of Chicago by an enigmatic gang. But the chase is metaphysical: the pursuers, who want Mickey to give an account of himself, are at least partly of his own imagining. The film is too self-consciously obscure, but its resonant images – Mickey trapped on stage by a dazzling spotlight, and an enormous sculpture going berserk of its own accord – continue to haunt the mind.

In outline, John Boorman's *Point Blank* (1967) is an absolutely straightforward thriller. After taking part in a robbery, Walker (Lee Marvin) is left for dead in the ruins of Alcatraz prison; he recovers, and sets about finding his former associates, killing them and recouping his share of the loot. But there is nothing straightforward about the way Boorman orders his material. He deliberately blurs the plot line by his use of flashbacks, flashes-forward, slow motion and elliptical editing, turning what could have been a formula thriller into a vision of urban chaos. Walker strides vindictively down an endless, sterile corridor; orgasmically empties a gun into his mistress's bed; and systematically smashes up a new convertible against the pillars of a Los Angeles freeway to obtain information from a car salesman. The shootings and beatings take place in a futuristic landscape of impersonal apartments and antiseptic office blocks. The animalistic Walker is virtually the only living person in a world of computers and credit cards: the morality of force is the only morality which prevails.

And it is the only morality which prevails in the same director's *Deliverance* (1972) in which four businessmen leave their comfortable urban environment to take a canoe trip up a wild river in the Appalachian mountains. They fight not only the river but each other as they seek deliverance from the nightmare in which they are trapped.

On pages 152–3
John Boorman's *Deliverance* (1972)

Conclusion

In *Harper* (UK title: *The Moving Target*), Paul Newman, the embittered private detective, notes that 'The bottom's full of nice people. Only cream and bastards rise.'

The rule applies equally well to the thrillers of the late sixties and early seventies. The heroes are, at the very least, submerged; alignment on one or other side of the law has become purely arbitrary. In *The French Connection*, the cops are as underhand, mean-spirited and ruthless as the dope-smugglers; Harry Callaghan, the detective in Don Siegel's *Dirty Harry* (1971), lives up to the film's title; Walker, in *Point Blank*, destroys people, cars and buildings with the same detached efficiency; even James Bond, nominally a hero, uses gutter tactics to overcome the comic-strip villains.

The flip attitude to violence and nihilistic philosophy of many of these films is, paradoxically, funny: the audience laughs, if uneasily, as the boot goes in. Villains, of course, have always engendered a certain amount of sympathy, but there is all the difference in the world between a bank robber defying the odds and the new-style hero-cum-villain whose only credo, like Mike Hammer's in *Kiss Me Deadly*, is: 'What's in it for me?'

The anarchic world of these thrillers is terrifying in its implications, arguably pornographic. But it is as alluring, in its devious way, as the innocent world of the forties romantic thriller where virtue inexorably triumphed. A sign of the times? Art reflecting life? It's the obvious conclusion to draw, and it says remarkably little for the times.

Stills

With acknowledgements to: Columbia-Warner, 20th Century-Fox, United Artists, MGM and Universal.

Index

Note : Numbers in italics refer to illustrations

A bout de souffle
  (*Breathless*) 143 ; *144–5*
Adams, Ken 45
Albert, Marvin H. 32
Albright, Lola 147
Aldrich, Robert 71, 111,
  114, 141 ; *112, 113, 142*
Alexander Nevsky 49
The Ambushers 48
The Anderson Tapes 139 ;
  139
Andrews, Dana *11*
d'Antoni, Philip 100
Any Number Can Win 137 ;
  138
Arabesque 75, 79–80, 85 ;
  78
The Asphalt Jungle 120–1,
  124
Attenborough, Richard 115
Axelrod, George 55

Bacall, Lauren 28
Balsam, Martin 103
Bande à part (UK : *The
  Outsiders* ; USA : *Band of
  Outsiders*) 143
Bass, Saul 137
Beatty, Warren *94–5, 133,
  150*
Begley, Ed 49
Belafonte, Harry 63 ; *63*
Belmondo, Jean-Paul 80,
  93, 142 ; *80, 144–5, 146*
Bendix, William 82
Bergman, Ingrid 36 ; *37*
The Best Man 55
The Big Sleep 22, 32, 35 ;
  23
The Big Snatch 137 ; *138*
The Big Steal 82 ; *83*
Billion-Dollar Brain 48–9 ;
  50
Bloom, Claire *50*
The Blue Dahlia 26 ; *27*

Boehm, Carl 107 ; *108–9*
Bogarde, Dirk 65 ; *65*
Bogart, Humphrey 22, 32,
  35 ; *23*
Bogart, Paul 32
Bogdanovitch, Peter 115,
  119 ; *119*
Boomerang 10–11 ; *11*
Boone, Richard 71
Boorman, John 151 ; *152–3*
The Boston Strangler 115 ;
  116–17
Boulting, Roy 110
Brackett, Leigh 22
Brahm, John 26 ; *26*
Brando, Marlon 71 ; *70*
The Brasher Doubloon
  (*UK : The High Window*)
  25–6 ; *26*
Breathless 143 ; *144–5*
Breck, Peter 115 ; *114*
Breen, Richard L. 32
Broca, Phillippe de 80 ; *80*
Broccoli, Albert 43–4, 48,
  54
Brooks, Richard 62, 93,
  132 ; *94–5, 133*
Brown, Drew Bundini 32
Buchan, John 75
Bullitt 90, 100 ; *90–1*
The Burglars 93 ; *92*
Burnett, W.R. 120
Burton, Richard 49, 52 ;
  51

The Cabinet of Dr Caligari
  54
Cagney, James 11 ; *12*
Caine, Michael 48, 125,
  127, 129–30 ; *49, 50, 129*
Calhern, Louis 120
Call Northside 777 13, 16 ;
  16, 17
Carreras, Michael *104*
Casino Royale 53–4 ; *53*

Le Cassé (*The Burglars*)
  93 ; *92*
Castle, William 107
Chabrol, Claude 48
Chandler, Raymond 22–7,
  28, 32, 35, 74
Charade 75–9 ; *76–7*
Circle of Deception 42
Citizen Kane 9
Le Clan des Siciliens (*The
  Sicilian Clan*) 130
Clement, René 147 ; *148–*
Cloak and Dagger 38 ; *38*
Clouzot, Henri-Georges
  58–9, 103 ; *58*
Cobb, Lee J. 71 ; *11, 72–3*
Coburn, James 45, 130 ;
  46
Collins, Joan *136*
Condon, Richard 55
*Confessions of a Counter-
  Spy* 40
Connery, Sean 43, 139 ;
  42, 44, 139
Conte, Richard *17*
Coogan's Bluff 96–7 ; *96*
Cool Breeze 121 ; *121*
Cooper, Gary 38 ; *38*
Corbett, Glenn 69
Cornered 81–2 ; *81*
Costa-Gavras 59 ; *60*
Cotten, Joseph 85, 111
The Counterfeit Traitor
  40–2 ; *41*
Crawford, Joan 111
The Crimson Kimono
  68–9 ; *69*
Crossfire 62 ; *62*
Cry of the City 16
Cul-de-Sac 147, 150 ; *147*
Curtis, Tony 115 ; *116–17*

Dassin, Jules 12–13, 39,
  80, 121, 124, 125 ; *13,
  122–3, 124–5*

Davies, Jack 127
Davis, Bette 111 ; *112, 113*
Davis, Carl 129–30 ; *129*
Dead-Heat on a Merry-Go-Round 130
The Deadly Affair 52
Dearden, Basil 63, 130 ; *64, 65, 132*
Deighton, Len 48
Deliverance 151 ; *152–3*
Delon, Alain 130, 137, 147 ; *138, 148–9*
Deneuve, Catherine 110
The Detective 65 ; *66–7*
Les Diaboliques 103, 111
Diamonds Are Forever 91 ; *44, 93*
Dillman, Bradford 42
Dirty Harry 154
Dmytryk, Edward 25, 62, 81 ; *24, 62, 81*
D.O.A. 82
Dollars (UK: *The Heist*) 93, 132 ; *94–5, 133*
Donat, Robert 75
Donen, Stanley 75, 79 ; *76–7, 78*
Dorléac, Françoise 150
Douglas, Gordon 32, 45, 65 ; *31, 39, 66–7*
Douglas, Kirk 57 ; *57*
Dr No 42–3 ; *42–3*
Duel 97 ; *97*
Dunaway, Fay 130

Eastwood, Clint 96–7 ; *96*
Edwards, Blake 29 ; *29*
Egan, Richard 132
Eisenstein, Sergei 49
Elg, Taina *75*
England, Barry 85
Exton, Clive 115
Eyes Without a Face 111 ; *110*

Fanatic 103
Farewell My Lovely 22, 81 ; *24*
Faulkner, William 23 *20–1, 98–9*
Feldman, Charles K. 54
Les Félins (UK: *The Love Cage* ; US: *Joy House*) 147 ; *148–9*
Figures in a Landscape 85

Finney, Albert 35
Fitzgerald, Geraldine 38
Fleischer, Richard 93, 115, 132 ; *116–17, 135*
Fonda, Jane 147
Forbes, Brian 129 ; *129*
Francis, Freddie *105*
Franju, Georges 111 ; *110*
Frankenheimer, John 55–7 ; *56, 57*
Frear, Stephen 35 ; *34*
The French Connection 19, 100, 154 ; *20–1, 98–9*
Friedkin, William 19, 100 ; *20–1, 98–9*
The Frightened City 16
Frobe, Gerd 45
Fuller, Samuel 40, 68, 115, 143 ; *40, 69, 114*
Funeral in Berlin 48
Furie, Sidney J. 48 ; *49*
Furthman, Jules 22

Gabin, Jean 130, 137
Gambit 125, 127
The Garment Center (UK: *The Garment Jungle*) 71 ; *72–3*
Garner, James 32
Gavin, John 48
Girard, Bernard 114, 130
Godard, Jean-Luc 143 ; *144–5, 146*
Goldman, William 28
Grant, Cary 7, 36, 74, 78–9 ; *37, 76–7*
Green, Janet 63
Greene, David 105–7 ; *106*
Greene, Graham 55, 85
Greenstreet, Sydney 35
Guest, Val 54 ; *53*
Gumshoe 35 ; *34*
Gunn 29 ; *29*
Guss, Jack 32

Hackman, Gene 100 ; *20–1*
Hamilton, Donald 45
Hamilton, Guy 48, 91 ; *44, 93*
Hammer Films 103–7
Hammett, Dashiell 32, 35
Harper (UK: *The Moving Target*) 28–9, 154 ; *28*
Harrington, Curtis 114

Harvey, Laurence 55 ; *56*
Hathaway, Henry 10, 11, 13, 137 ; *10, 12, 14–15, 17, 136*
Havilland, Olivia De 111
Hawks, Howard 22 ; *23*
Hawn, Goldie *94–5*
Hayden, Sterling 120, 124
Hayworth, Rita 140
He Walked By Night 17
The Heist 93, 132 ; *94–5, 133*
Hepburn, Audrey 78–9
Herrman, Bernard 103
Heston, Charlton 140
Hickox, Doug 93
The High Window 25–6 ; *26*
Hitchcock, Alfred 7, 36, 52, 74, 75, 78, 101–3 ; *37, 52, 102*
Holden, William 42 ; *41*
L'Homme de Rio (*That Man from Rio*) 80 ; *80*
The Hot Rock (UK: *How to Steal a Diamond in Four Uneasy Lessons*) 127–9 ; *127, 128*
The House on 92nd Street 9–10, 12–13, 36 ; *10*
How to Steal a Diamond in Four Uneasy Lessons 127–9 ; *127, 128*
Hughes, Ken 54 ; *53*
Hush, Hush Sweet Charlotte 111, 113 ; *113*
Huston, John 22, 54, 120 ; *53*

I Married a Communist 39
I Was a Communist for the FBI 39 ; *39*
In Like Flint 45
Indagine su un cittadine al di sopra di ogni sospetto (*Investigation of a Citizen Above Suspicion*) 59–61 ; *61*
The Ipcress File 48 ; *49*

Janssen, David 30 ; *30*
Jewison, Norman 130 ; *131*
John, Errol *64*
Joy House 147 ; *148–9*

Karloff, Boris 119
Karlson, Phil 48 ; *47*
Kazan, Elia 10–11, 16, 69,
  71 ; *11, 18, 70*
Keighley, William 16
Kennedy, George *76–7*
Kiss Me Deadly 141–3,
  154 ; *142*
Kiss of Death 13 ; *14–15*
Krasker, Robert 85
Kulik, Buzz 30 ; *30*

Ladd, Alan 26, 36 ; *27, 37*
The Lady from Shanghai
  29, 140 ; *141*
Lady in Cement 32
Lady in the Lake 25 ; *25*
Lancaster, Burt 57 ; *57*
Lang, Fritz 38, 48 ; *38*
The Last Run 93
Le Carré, John 49, 52
The League of Gentlemen
  130 ; *132*
Lee, Jack 42
Lehman, Ernest 74
Leigh, Janet 7, 101
Levin, Henry 48
The Line-Up 90
Lloyd, Sue *49*
Lloyd-Webber, Andrew 35
Lom, Herbert 127
The Looking-Glass War
  52
Loren, Sophia 79 ; *78*
Losey, Joseph 39, 85
The Love Cage 147 ; *148–9*
Lovejoy, Frank *39*
Lumet, Sidney 52, 139 ;
  139

McCallum, David 45
McCarthy, Senator Joseph
  39
Macdonald, Ross 28
MacDougall, Ronald 62
McDowell, Malcolm 85
McEvoy, Earl 16
MacGowran, Jack 150
McGrath, Joe 54 ; *53*
MacLaine, Shirley 127
McQueen, Steve 90, 130 ;
  131
The Maltese Falcon 22

The Man from UNCLE 45
Man on a String (UK :
  Confessions of a
  Counter-Spy) 40
The Manchurian Candidate
  55–7 ; *56*
Maniac 103 ; *104*
Mann, Anthony 17
Mann, Daniel 45 ; *46*
March, Frederic 57 ; *57*
March of Time 9
Marie-Chantal contre le
  Docteur Kha 48
Marks, Leo 107, 110
Marlowe 32
Marshall, George 26 ; *27*
Martin, Dean 48 ; *47*
Marton, Pierre *see* Stone,
  Peter
Marvin, Lee 132, 151 ; *88,*
  89, 135
Mason, James 85 ; *84*
Massey, Anna *108–9*
Maté, Rudolf 82
A Matter of Life and
  Death (US : *Stairway to*
  Heaven) 107
Matthews, Kerwin 48 ;
  72–3, 104
Matthau, Walter 79
Mature, Victor 132 ; *15*
Medford, Don 45
Meeker, Ralph 141 ; *142*
Melodie en sous-sol (UK :
  The Big Snatch ; US :
  Any Number Can Win)
  137 ; *138*
Mickey One 151 ; *150*
Milestone, Lewis 135, 137 ;
  134
Mitchum, Robert 82 ; *83*
Montand, Yves *60*
Montgomery, George 26
Montgomery, Robert 25 ;
  25
More, Kenneth 75 ; *75*
Morris, Oswald 52
Mostel, Zero 129 ; *128*
The Moving Target 28–9,
  154 ; *28*
Murder My Sweet (UK :
  Farewell My Lovely) 22,
  81 ; *24*
Murderers' Row 48

Naish, J. Carrol *135*
The Naked City 12–13, 80 ;
  13
Neame, Ronald 125
Newman, Paul 29, 154
Night and the City 13, 80
Niven, David 54
No Way to Treat a Lady
  115 ; *118*
North by Northwest 7,
  74–5, 78, 85
Notorious 36 ; *37*

O'Brien, Edmond 82, 85
O'Kelly, Tim *119*
Ocean's 11 135, 137 ; *134*
Odd Man Out 85 ; *84*
On the Waterfront 71 ; *70*
OSS 36 ; *37*
Our Man Flint 45 ; *46*
The Outsiders 143

Palance, Jack *18*
Palmer, Lilli 38
Panic in the Streets 16,
  17–19 ; *18*
Paranoiac 103 ; *105*
Parks, Gordon 32 ; *33,*
  86–7
Parrish, Robert 54 ; *53*
Patrick, Nigel *64*
Peck, Gregory 79 ; *78*
Peeping Tom 107 ; *108–9*
Penn, Arthur 151 ; *150*
Perkins, Anthony 101 ; *10.*
Peter Gunn 29
Petri, Elio 59–61 ; *61*
Pichel, Irving 36 ; *37*
Pick-up on South Street
  40 ; *40*
Pierrot le Fou 143 ; *146*
Pierce, Stack *121*
Pierson, Frank 52
Point Blank 151, 154
Polanski, Roman 110, 147
  150 ; *147*
Pollack, Barry 121 ; *121*
Portman, Eric 129–30
Powell, Dick 25, 80–2 ; *24*
  81, 82
Powell, Michael 107, 110
  108–9
Pleasance, Donald 150 ;
  147
Preminger, Otto 56

essburger, Emeric 107
ime Cut 85 ; 88, 89
ycho 7, 101–3, 105, 107
10, 111, 115 ; 102

ayle, Anna 54

ft, George 54
d Shoes 107
ed, Carol 85 ; 84
ed, Oliver 105 ; 105, 106
lph, Michael 63
mick, Lee 65
pulsion 110–11, 147
ynolds, Debbie 114
ifi (Du Rififi chez les
ommes) 121, 124, 125 ;
22–3

chie, Michael 85 ; 88, 89
t, Martin 49, 52 ; 51
bbery 90–1
binson, Edward G. 137 ;
36
bson, Flora 106
chemont, Louis de
–11
undtree, Richard 32 ;
3, 86–7
le, Janice 34
ssell, Ken 48–9 ; 50
an, Robert 62

Jacques, Raymond 121
Salaire de la Peur (The
Vages of Fear) 58–9 ;
8–9
tzman, Harry 43–4, 48,
4
ophire 63 ; 64
rgent, Alvin 127
haffner, Franklin 55
ob, Edith 110
ott George C. 93
aton, George 40–2 ; 41
gal, George 127
lers, Peter 54
rvais, Jean 124
ven Days in May 55,
7–8 ; 57
ven Thieves 137 ; 136
aft 32
aft's Big Score 32–4, 85 ;
3, 86–7
arif, Omar 92
aw, Robert 85

Sherman, Vincent 71 ;
72–3
Shock Corridor 115 ; 114
The Shuttered Room
105–7 ; 106
The Sicilian Clan 130
Side Street 17
Siegel, Don 82, 90, 96,
154 ; 83, 96
The Silencers 45 ; 47
Silliphant, Stirling 32
The Simple Art of Murder 74
Sinatra, Frank 32, 65, 135 ;
31, 66–7, 134
Siodmak, Robert 16
Sitting Target 93, 96
Sloane, Everett 140
Smight, Jack 28, 115 ; 28,
118
Spacek, Sissy 88
Spielberg, Steven 97 ; 97
Spillane, Mickey 141
The Spy Who Came in
from the Cold 49, 52 ; 51
Stafford, Frederick 48
Stairway to Heaven 107
Stander, Lionel 150
Steiger, Rod 115, 137 ;
118, 136
Steiner, Max 35
Stevens, Craig 29
Stevenson, Robert 82 ; 82
Stewart, James 16 ; 16, 17
Stone, Peter (Pierre
Marton) 78, 80
Straitjacket 107
The Street With No Name 16
Syms, Sylvia 65 ; 65

10 Rillington Place 115
13 Rue Madeleine 11, 36 ;
12
20th Century-Fox 11, 19
Targets 115, 119 ; 119
The Testament of Dr
Mabuse 48
That Man From Rio 80 ; 80
The Third Man 85
The Thirty-Nine Steps 75 ;
75
Thomas, Ralph 75 ; 75
The Thomas Crown Affair
130–2 ; 131
Tidyman, Ernest 32

Tiffin, Pamela 28
Le Tigre aime la chair
fraîche 48
To the ends of the Earth
82 ; 82
To Trap a Spy 45
Tony Rome 30–2 ; 31
Topaz 52–3 ; 52
Topkapi 125 ; 124–5, 126
Torn Curtain 52–3
Toth, André De 40
Touch of Evil 140
Twisted Nerve 110

Ustinov, Peter 125 ; 126

Vaughn, Robert 45
Verneuil, Henri 93, 130,
137 ; 92, 138
Victim, 65 ; 65
Violent Saturday 132 ; 135
Volonte, Gian-Marie 61

The Wages of Fear 58–9 ;
58–9
Wagner, Robert 28
Walsh, Raoul 9
Warning Shot 30 ; 30
Weaver, Dennis 97 ; 97
Welch, Raquel 32
Welles, Orson, 9, 29, 54,
85, 140–1 ; 53, 141
Werker, Alfred 17
Whatever Became of Aunt
Helen? 114
Whatever Happened to
Baby Jane? 111–114 ; 112
White, Lionel 143
White Heat 9
Whitmore, James 120
Whoever Slew Auntie Roo?
114
Widmark, Richard 13, 17,
19 ; 14
The World, the Flesh and
the Devil 62–3 ; 63
The Wrecking Crew 48

Yates, Peter 90–1, 127 ;
90, 127
Les Yeux sans visage (Eyes
Without a Face) 111 ; 110
Young, Terence 42 ; 42

Z 59 ; 60

STUDIO VISTA | DUTTON PICTUREBACKS
edited by David Herbert

European domestic architecture by Sherban Cantacuzino
Great modern architecture by Sherban Cantacuzino
Modern houses of the world by Sherban Cantacuzino

European sculpture by David Bindman
Florentine sculpture by Anthony Bettram
Michelangelo by Anthony Bertram
Modern sculpture by Alan Bowness

The Aesthetic Movement by Robin Spencer
Art deco by Bevis Hillier
Art nouveau by Mario Amaya
The Bauhaus by Gillian Naylor
Cartoons and caricatures by Bevis Hillier
Dada by Kenneth Coutts-Smith
De Stijl by Paul Overy
Futurism by Jane Rye
Indian art by Philip Rawson
An introduction to Optical art by Cyril Barrett
Lovers in art by G. S. Whittet
Modern graphics by Keith Murgatroyd
Modern prints by Pat Gilmour
Pop art: object and image by Christopher Finch
The Pre-Raphaelites by John Nicoll
Spanish painting by John Moffitt
Surrealism by Roger Cardinal and Robert Stuart Short
Symbolists and Decadents by John Milner
William Blake: the artist by Ruthven Todd

Modern ballet by John Percival
Modern ceramics by Geoffrey Beard
Modern glass by Geoffrey Beard
The story of cybernetics by Maurice Trask
The world of Diaghilev by John Percival

Andy Warhol by Peter Gidal
Charlie Chaplin: early comedies by Isabel Quigly
The films of Alfred Hitchcock by George Perry
French film by Roy Armes
The great funnies by David Robinson
Greta Garbo by Raymond Durgnat and John Kobal
Movie monsters by Denis Gifford
New cinema in Britain by Roger Manvell
New cinema in Eastern Europe by Alistair Whyte
New cinema in Europe by Roger Manvell
New cinema in the USA by Roger Manvell
Science fiction film by Denis Gifford
The silent cinema by Liam O'Leary
The Thriller by Brian Davis